להו"ו

This book
belongs to:

ISBN 978-1-68025-691-8

FELDHEIM PUBLISHERS
POB 34549 / Jerusalem, Israel
208 Airport Executive Park
Nanuet, NY 10954
www.feldheim.com

Distributed in Europe by:
LEHMANNS
+44-0-191-430-0333
info@lehmanns.co.uk
www.lehmanns.co.uk

Distributed in Australia by:
GOLDS WORLD OF JUDAICA
+613 95278775
info@golds.com.au
www.golds.com.au

Printed in China

Body Is

By Alyssa Goldwater & Chanie Kamman

Illustrated by Dafne Zivan

FELDHEIM

DEDICATED TO

My beautiful children,
with the deepest wish that they always shine brightly and embrace their own unique beauty, strength, and purpose.

The Lubavitcher Rebbe zy"a,
who recognized the inherent goodness in every soul, and loved every person unconditionally.

Chanie Kamman

DEDICATED TO

All women, girls, men, or boys who have ever felt shame, guilt, ugly, less-than, or unworthy because of the body Hashem gave them.

Everyone who is recovering from, or bound by, the diseases and diet culture that make us believe that there is only one acceptable body type.

My precious children, Miri and Azi. I will fight every single day to ensure you ALWAYS know how beautiful and perfect you are, inside and out.

And to myself. I am so proud of you.

Hashem never makes mistakes.
We are all perfect, exactly the way we are.

Alyssa Goldwater

SPONSOR

Dear Jewish women and girls everywhere:

Sometimes, as I watch you from the stage, from afar, singing with your friends and dancing with such emotion, I also see the effort you put into facing the challenges of today.

As I hear you sing, I wonder if you know just how much you matter. I wonder if you know just how special you are. I wonder if you know that Hashem made your body strong, beautiful, and full of endless possibilities.

And while I wonder, I also hope. I hope you know that there's no one else like you in the entire world! I hope you know to celebrate every part of you because you are perfect in your own special way. I hope you know that you are worthy of love, joy, and all the kindness in the world!

Most of all, I hope you that when you read this book — and every day — you know that you are always beautiful, just the way you are.

All my love,

Shaindy Plotzker

Every body is different,
No two will look the same.
Think about what makes you you;
It's not just in your name.

Yeshiva Tiferes Yaakov

Notice people's colors,
Their skin, their eyes and hair.
All sizes, accents, funny laughs,
And clothes they choose to wear.

Every body is different!

Every body is just right,
There's no specific way,
To dance, or swim, or throw a ball,
All styles are okay.

Hashem has made you with great care,
Each part of you He chose.
You're made just right the way you are —
Your head down to your toes.

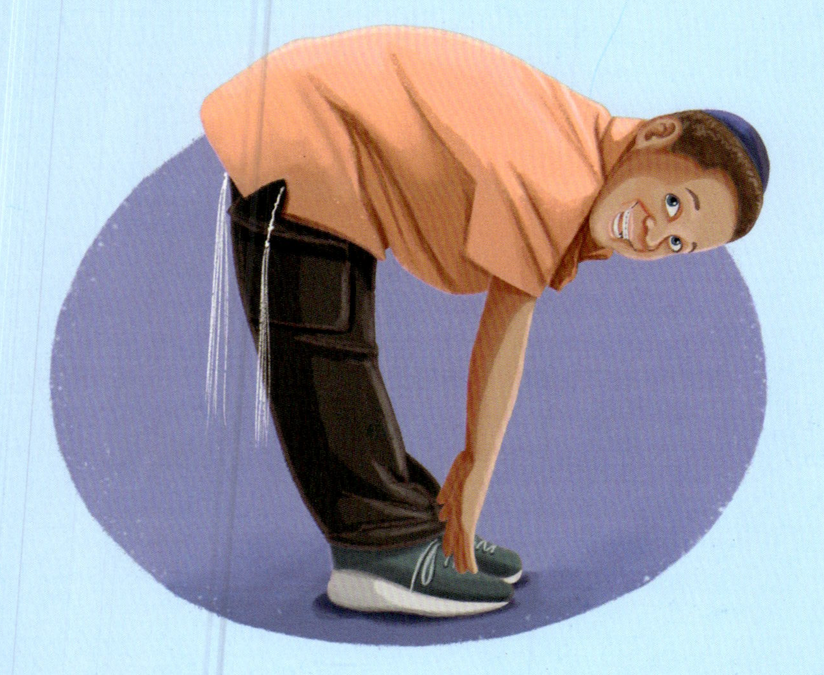

Every body is just right!

Every body is beautiful,
Whether thin, fat, short, or tall,
With many different body types,
There's beauty in them all.

Friendly, honest, kind, and smart,
There's so much more to you.
Your thoughtful mind and heart that loves,
Inside has beauty, too!

Every body is special,
It's unique and that's what's cool.
When you're yourself, you shine the most,
At home, the park, or school.

Hashem decided long ago,
The world was made for you,
You're needed here, that's very clear,
For all that you can do.

Every body is special!

Every body is made up of parts,
That together make us whole.
Thoughts and feelings of every type,
And a very holy soul.

Every single piece of you,
Plays a big, important role.
Yes, ALL parts of you matter,
To accept yourself's the goal.

Every body is made up of parts!

Every body is worthy,
Which means that you should be,
Respected, valued, and held dear,
In every size — that's key.

When looking in the mirror,
The image that you see,
Is lovable no matter what,
That's a guarantee!

Every body is worthy!

Every body is a home for Hashem,
With a holy neshamah in it.
When you eat, learn, or even sleep,
Hashem's with you every minute.

He made a special mitzvah,
To always keep in mind:
Our bodies we must treat with care
However it's designed.

Every body is a home for Hashem!

Sometimes the world will tell you,
You must look a certain way.

"Your nose is weird, your laugh's too loud,
Your round belly's not okay."

But you should know, dear child,
For sure, without a doubt,
You're special, worthy, made just right —
And beautiful...

... *inside and out.*

בס"ד

A Parent's Guide to Positive Body Image and Emotional Wellness in Kids

BY RACHEL TUCHMAN, LMHC

RETHINKING HEALTH

I am sure I speak for many parents when I say that one of our top parenting goals includes having kids who are physically, spiritually, and emotionally healthy. At the same time, we are constantly being told that health is comprised of only two very specific things — what we eat and how our bodies look — when in reality it is composed of many more complex and highly individual factors.

A lot of the research on health tells us that our mental and emotional well-being have a greater impact on physical health and longevity than gym workouts, BMI (body mass index), or even how many fruits and vegetables we consume. In order to achieve true health, we need to stop focusing solely on the size and gravitational pull of our bodies and instead prioritize mental well-being, physical environments, healthy behaviors, and meaningful relationships.

THE HARM OF FOCUSING SOLELY ON BODY SIZE AND WEIGHT

Focusing on bodies, weight, or only eating "healthy" foods causes harm to people's well-being by moralizing food and creating feelings of guilt and shame. Removing certain foods from the home because of temptation or fear creates guilt, confusion, and mistrust. Similarly, when we make comments on kids' weight, shape, or eating habits, it can send a message to kids that their bodies are "wrong," which can cause them to feel rejected, unloved, and unsafe in their skin. Ultimately, a healthy relationship with food and one's own body is far more important than any food ingredient or form of exercise.

As Jews, we understand the power of prioritizing and connecting with something more meaningful and spiritual, beyond the physical. While we do not shy away from the physical, we know that everything in this world can be used as a vehicle to enhance and improve our spiritual connection to Hashem and our *avodas Hashem*.

EXAMINING YOUR OWN BELIEFS

Kids learn more from our actions than our words so it's important to lead by example!

The way we talk about food and our own bodies has a profound influence on how kids view their own. Consider these questions: Do you label certain foods as good or bad? Do you judge and associate bigger bodies with moral choices? Do you talk badly about yourself when looking in the mirror? Do you view thin bodies as better or more attractive? What do you say about people in bigger bodies? Did you struggle with weight as a child? How does dieting feel? What is your current relationship with your body, food, and exercise? Do you think "fat" is a bad word?

It's important to remember that the messages we send, intentionally or not, influence our children's developing sense of self-worth and their relationship with their bodies for years to come.

THE IMPACT OF SOCIETY ON SELF-WORTH

Sadly, at times the world will tell our kids very early on that their bodies aren't "good enough," and have them chase a wholly unachievable and ever-changing standard that is often focused on physical appearance and weight. This pursuit can put them at risk for lifelong struggles with food, their bodies, and their self-worth.

Negative body image is associated with poorer mental and physical health and greater psychological distress. Children with heightened body dissatisfaction are less likely to join a sports team, participate in spontaneous play, raise their hand in class, or engage socially. Growing body dissatisfaction can lower the quality of life and is a risk factor for the development of eating disorders — which are the deadliest form of mental illnesses and are on the rise.

Within the Jewish community, we have alarmingly higher-than-average rates of eating disorders. One study estimated that the prevalence of eating disorders among Jewish women is 50% higher than the general population. Factors like communal pressure, high achievement standards, food-centered holidays, and anti-fat bias or weight stigma contribute to these issues.

To counter these pressures, education and prevention are the greatest tools we can utilize. Instead of allowing society or health professionals to tell us to focus solely on shrinking or changing our kids' bodies, we can take a different path. We can teach our kids to love and respect themselves just as they are. We can help them trust their innate cues, honor their hunger, expose them to all types of foods, and enjoy the pleasures of eating without guilt or shame. We can show them the joy of movement and how it is a wonderful tool to enhance our physical and mental health. We can teach them that health is multifaceted and not defined by appearance. All bodies are good bodies, healthy people come in all shapes and sizes, and everyone is worthy of connection, love, and respect, regardless of their size.

TRUSTING OUR BODIES

Hashem, in His infinite wisdom, created humans to be born knowing what their bodies need. As new parents, we trusted newborns' cries to tell us if they were hungry, full, tired, or uncomfortable. Although children are born as intuitive eaters, over time they are taught by adults to not trust their natural inner cues anymore:

"You had enough now."

"One more bite, you didn't eat enough."

"Finish what's on your plate if you want dessert."

"You don't need that, you already had...."

Children are taught that certain foods are "junk" or "poison", and that other foods are "better" and "healthier." When kids want "bad" foods, they may feel guilt and shame, internalizing the message that they are bad too. These mostly well-intentioned actions tell a child: "I'll tell you what is good for your body, no matter how you feel. You can't be trusted to know what you need."

What I am *not* saying is that your kids should have free reign in the snack drawers and that they can decide what to eat. What I am saying is that when we approach our children's hunger with curiosity and respect, we help them build self-trust and learn to be thoughtful as to what their body actually needs.

SHIFTING FOCUS TO HEALTHY BEHAVIORS AND SUPPORTING GENERAL WELLBEING

Are there times when the relationship with food or weight is a concern? Yes, and the solution is not to prescribe weight loss or restriction. Obsession with certain foods isn't healthy, but we need to consider the reason behind this and respond accordingly. This might mean increasing access in a respectful way to decrease anxiety around that particular food. Sudden weight changes in *either* direction can be concerning too, yet we celebrate and praise one while panicking about and shaming the other. Instead, focusing on behaviors that support overall health without focusing on weight brings far greater benefits in the long run. This can include increasing fruit and vegetable intake for your family (not just one child), incorporating more movement, improving sleep, managing stress by teaching a variety of coping skills, quitting smoking, and reducing alcohol consumption.

Instead of teaching kids that health is all about their body size, we can:

- Help them learn to trust their bodies and hunger cues, regardless of size.
- Help them find enjoyable movement and physical activities.
- Offer a variety of foods in tastes and textures, and consider their preferences.
- Let them eat until they are truly satisfied, without judgment.

- Don't label foods as good or bad. All foods have a time and place.
- Neutralize the word "fat" in your home and let your kids know that we don't use it as an insult.
- Teach them that commenting on people's bodies is never okay and that we are all so much more than our bodies.
- Teach them about body diversity and the natural changes to expect during adolescence, including the necessary weight gain.

What our children need from us is love, support, and understanding that their worth is not connected to their body size. We all want to set our kids up for success, and the best way to do that is by helping them develop a healthy relationship with themselves, regardless of what their bodies look like. Ultimately, as the pages in this book relay, it's important to remember that our children are made in Hashem's image, and it is our obligation and honor to nurture, care for, and educate them with love.

Rachel Tuchman, LMHC is an HAES (Health at Every Size) aligned clinician who works with eating disorders and disordered eating. In addition, Rachel dedicates a lot of her time out of office to educating parents and kids on the importance of body respect and the behaviors that truly honor our health. She currently offers services in her Cedarhurst, NY, office.

About the authors

Chanie Kamman, a mother of seven young children, is passionate about raising kids with respect, emotional wellness, and joyful Judaism.

Recognizing a void of Jewish resources for kids on emotional health, she took the initiative to create them herself. Her popular children's books include *Me & My Feelings*, *The Friend That Stayed*, and *I Messed Up*, with hopes of writing more during nap time, between homework crises, and fueled by a steady supply of lukewarm coffee.

Together with her husband and children, Chanie is a proud Chabad Shlucha in Stamford, CT.

Alyssa Goldwater has created a community and support network of more than 200,000 women across the world by having hard conversations about difficult topics, such as mental health, the dangers of diet culture, and the unspoken struggles of motherhood. She keeps people laughing with her sarcastic take on life, and helps women feel supported and not alone.

Along with other movers and shakers in the Anti-Diet Culture, Plus Size Advocacy, and Eating Disorder Recovery movements, Alyssa is helping to redefine beauty and "health" standards by pushing the boundaries of what society deems as "acceptable."

Alyssa lives in Chicago, IL with her husband and two children. As a Digital Influencer behind the lifestyle brand "A Glass of Goldwater," you can follow her by visiting www.aglassofgoldwater.com

Also by Chanie Kamman and Illustrated by Dafne Zivan

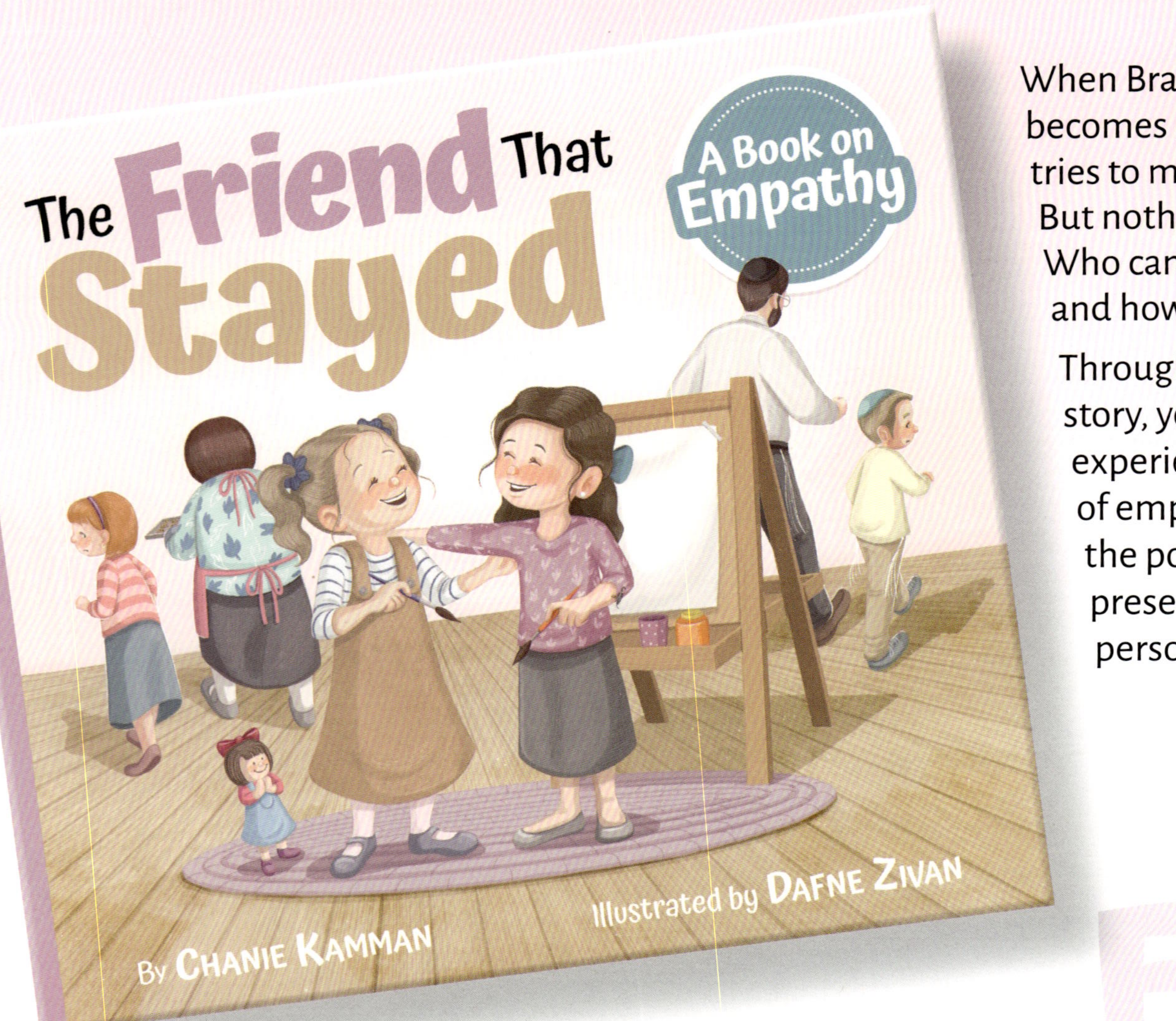

When Bracha's painting becomes ruined, everyone tries to make her feel better. But nothing seems to work. Who can comfort Bracha — and how?

Through this beautiful story, your children will experience the benefits of empathy and learn the power of being fully present for another person's experience.

Why didn't Avi feel better, even after his friend said, "I'm sorry"?

I Messed Up helps children understand the real meaning of *teshuvah*. Join Avi as he discovers and experiences the power of sincere repair with others — and with Hashem.

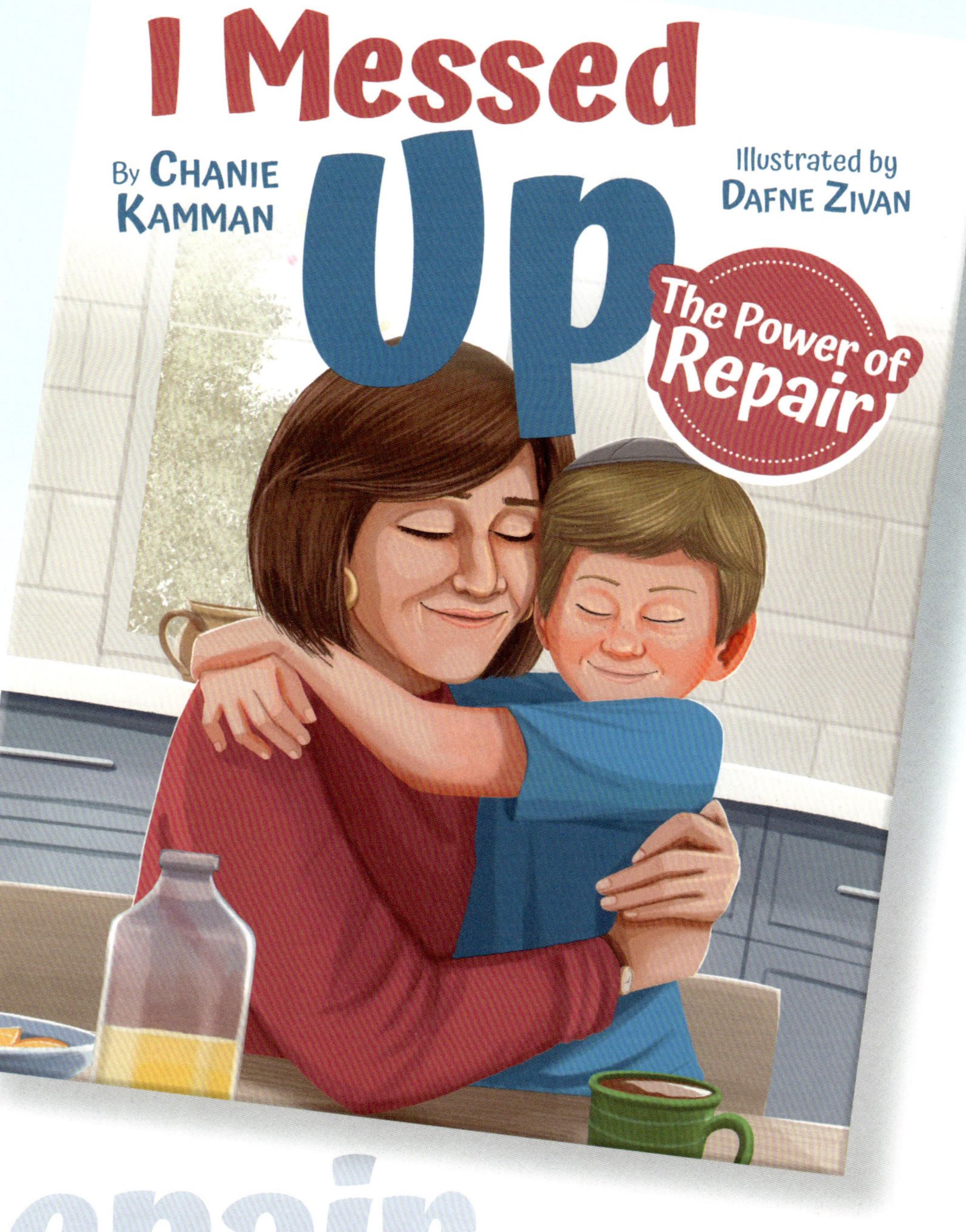